simple summer

a recipe for cooking and entertaining with ease

JONATHAN BARDZIK

These people's photography make this book beautiful:

Sam Armocido—food photography
Santos Photography & Design—event photography
Jenny Lehman | www.jennylehman.com—Eastern Market produce

For more about the beautiful plants and flowers, check out:

Angela Treadwell-Palmer and Plants Nouveau

 New Plants | New Markets | New Solutions

Plants Nouveau is a company about plants, fueled by the introduction of novel, innovative selections from passionate plant people. Royalties collected by Plants Nouveau are shared with the plant's originator and re-invested into the program's clever, innovative marketing efforts.
www.plantsnouveau.com

Garry Grueber and Cultivaris

cultivaris

Cultivaris North America LLC is a product development and idea management company operating in the global plant industry. Working with plant breeders from around the world, we try to bring out-of-the-box thinking to the horticultural industry. We believe that innovation is the key to growth and success in the global plant market.
www.cultivaris.com

Design: Lookout Design, Inc. | www.lookoutdesign.com

Editorial development and creative design support by Ascent:
www.itsyourlifebethere.com

For Mom, Dad, Katie and Alec,
and my husband Jason.

If summer had more days
I would spend each of them with you.
Probably cooking.

celebrate: *simple foods for special events*

party! *bold flavors for bright summer days*

too darn hot: *cool cooking for summer's dog days*

fall's first: *fresh flavors for changing seasons*

SIMPLE SUMMER:

My parents opened their garden center, Tarnów Nursery, the year I was born. For most of my life it has dominated their schedules, as a small business often does. However, ten years ago, the summer I moved to DC, I started getting these calls.

"Good morning," they said, their mobile phone on speaker. "We're taking today off. We're sitting in the car at the end of the driveway, trying to decide whether to turn left or right."

After a few of these calls, I realized the direction they chose didn't matter. They were taking the day to be together, and nothing was more important than that.

This is what I love most about summer. With warm weather, soft breezes, gardens in flower and markets filled with farm-fresh produce, the details are unimportant. As long as you get outside with people who bring you joy, it's going to be a wonderful day—

whether a grand celebration, or a lazy afternoon.

Summer cooking is just as simple. Vegetables, fresh from the garden, do most of the work. Zucchini shines with little more than butter and cilantro. A simple vinaigrette with 25-year-aged balsamic transforms tomatoes. Grill marks are the perfect garnish for a salt-and-pepper-seasoned steak.

My parents' days off together often began by turning up the road that runs next to my family's farm, where the speed limit is 25 mph. My Dad has always loved that sign. I do, too. It's the speed of summer. Simple. There's no rush.

celebrate:

simple foods for special events

WHAT WE REMEMBER MOST:

It was late May, my family's garden center business was in full swing, and Mom and Dad were heading home from another long day.

"We're tired," Mom said over the phone.

I had spent the afternoon preparing a special dinner. I set the table with white linens and collected flowers and large leaves from around our farmhouse, placing them in a jumble of clear glass vases amidst a half-dozen candlesticks. China, flatware and glasses were carefully chosen and placed.

We remember most, however, what happened as Mom and Dad pulled into the driveway.

I had placed stereo speakers in my third floor bedroom windows and hit "play" on Billie Holiday. Mom and Dad turned off their Dodge Caravan. Tired and still wound up from work, they stepped out onto the pea stone drive as I walked from the house carrying a tray. On it sat three

glasses of white wine. Billie sang, "You go to my head…"

I invited Mom and Dad to grab a glass and follow me through the gardens by the carriage shed. We walked behind the barns and around into the back yard. By the time we stepped into the house for dinner, we were relaxed, laughing easily.

Simple summer celebrations— anniversaries and birthdays, weekends

away with friends, flags and fireworks—are easy and elegant. A light sundress or white cotton shirt counts as dressing up. Tea lights and gardens in flower take care of the decorations. Fresh ingredients relieve the burden of hours of cooking. It's summer, and there's nothing more important to do tonight than kick back, listen to some good music, and celebrate with family and friends.

WHAT TO DRINK: RAISE A GLASS

Bubbly—nothing says "celebration" like the pop of a cork. Save the Veuve Cliquot for a special evening and make every night an event with a bottle of Cava or Prosecco, the sparkling wines of Spain and Italy.

Wine—Rosé has a bad rap. Saccharine bottles of White Zinfandel and sweet fruit infusions lack the subtlety and depth generally appreciated in wine. Good rosé, traditionally dry, crisp and served chilled, is the perfect wine for summer nights and summer foods. It has enough muscle to serve alongside steak, but won't overpower the sweetest corn or zucchini.

Cocktails—Classic cocktails rest easy in the hand on a summer evening and gin makes even the hottest summer night feel cooler. Mix up a classic gin and tonic with lime or cucumber. Get adventurous and muddle basil with sugar for a batch of gin mojitos.

MUSIC: SET THE MOOD

Summer celebrations are easy and relaxed. This playlist works from when the cork pops on your first bottle of champagne until the tea lights flicker out.

Billie Holiday—*You Go to My Head*
The Sundays—*Summertime*
Best Coast—*Summer Mood*
Prince—*Raspberry Beret*
Fleetwood Mac—*Songbird*
Pizzicato Five—*The Girl From Ipanema*
Peggy Lee—*The Boy From Ipanema*
Lily Frost—*Keeps on Raining*
Nina Simone—*Love Me or Leave Me*
Ella Fitzgerald—*Fascinatin' Rhythm*
Parov Stelar—*Booty Swing*
Tape Five—*Señorita Bonita*

JONATHAN BARDZIK

Tip: Fat adds flavor and moisture. Buying 90% lean beef
may save you a few calories, but it results in a dry,
dull burger. Balance it out with a light lunch!

Tip: To easily slice soft bleu cheeses, place in the freezer
for 20 minutes first. If not using right away, place the
slices in a single layer on parchment or wax paper.

mushroom bleu bacon burger

Makes 4 large burgers

Rich sautéed mushrooms, mild Humboldt Fog bleu goat cheese and smoky bacon dress up this burger for the most special celebrations, or just barbecuing barefoot in the backyard. If there's not juice running down your chin, you're doing it wrong!

Ingredients:

  8 slices thick cut bacon

  2 cups thinly sliced Shitake mushrooms

  1/4 cup Madeira wine or brandy

  2 pounds ground beef—ask for 80% lean

  2 eggs, lightly beaten

  1/4 cup parsley, chopped

  4 Kaiser rolls

  1/4 pound baby spinach

  1/4 pound Humboldt Fog or other mild bleu cheese, sliced

Directions:

- Fry bacon in a 12" skillet over medium-low heat until crispy, flipping once, about 5-6 minutes. Remove to paper towels to drain.

- Pour off bacon fat, leaving 2 tbs in the pan. Return pan to medium heat and add mushrooms, cooking until golden brown on edges, about 6 minutes.

- Add Madeira to mushrooms, scraping up brown bits and cook until reduced. Season to taste with salt and pepper. Reserve.

- Mix together ground beef, eggs and parsley. Season with salt and pepper and form into four large patties.

- Heat your grill to medium-high and grill burgers just off to the side of the coals. These are big patties, so you'll probably cook them for 5-7 minutes a side for medium rare.

- When the burgers come off the grill, let them rest for five minutes, tented with foil, while you lightly toast the buns.

- Layer bun bottoms with spinach, bacon and burgers. Top each with a slice of cheese, sautéed mushrooms and bun top.

SUMMER'S BLANK SLATE

Burgers are a tabula rasa in beef. Rich and smoky on toasted bread, they can handle anything from sweet relishes and fruit to savory cheeses and sauces. The fatty beef balances heat from chiles and the bitterness of garden-fresh greens like oak leaf lettuce and lemony sorrel. Dress it down or gussy it up. What ever you top, stuff or slather your burger with, have fun!

JONATHAN BARDZIK

TIP: If you're not using fresh corn right away, refrigerate it as soon as you get home from the farm or market. This will preserve the sugars, keeping the flavor light and sweet. Corn tastes its best within 48 hours.

TIP: Tomato seeds are hard, bitter and surrounded by water, qualities we often try to avoid in recipes like some salsas and this creamy, smooth soup. To quickly seed a tomato, cut it in quarters and scoop the seeds out with your finger.

corn and tomato bisque

Serves 6

Sweet corn and rich cream get a bright burst from the acid in fresh summer tomatoes and a finishing splash of sherry vinegar. The corn's starches reduce the need for lots of cream, keeping this soup a nice light, summer weight.

Ingredients:

4 ears of butter and sugar or bi-color corn, kernels removed

2 tbs olive oil

1 medium onion, diced

2 cloves of garlic, finely minced

2 large tomatoes, seeded and diced

4 cups chicken or vegetable stock

1/4 cup heavy cream

White pepper

Freshly grated nutmeg

Sherry vinegar

Directions:

- Spread corn on a baking sheet and roast in a 400 degree oven until edges are golden brown, about 5 minutes.

- Warm 2 tbs olive oil over medium heat in a 4 quart soup pot. Add onions and sauté until softened and translucent, about 5 minutes. Add garlic and cook 30 seconds longer until fragrant.

- Add tomatoes to soup pot and cook until softened, about 5 minutes.

- Add toasted corn kernels to tomato mixture along with chicken or vegetable stock. Bring soup to a simmer, and cook for 5 minutes longer, allowing flavors to blend.

- Remove 1/2 cup of solids. Purée remaining soup with an immersion blender or food processor.

- Add cream along with reserved solids, and stir through. Season to taste with pepper, freshly grated nutmeg, a splash of vinegar and salt.

PUTTING IT TOGETHER:

Celebrating the two of you—an anniversary dinner... for *any* anniversary!

Like the two of you, these dishes are better together. Make the butter ahead of time. That way, when you suddenly remember it's your anniversary at 5:00 pm, you can grab steaks and some bubbly on the way home.

» Corn and Tomato Bisque

» Grilled Porterhouse or tuna steaks with Cilantro, Lime, Cumin Compound Butter

» Blueberry Balsamic Spinach Salad

THIS IS WHAT YOU TAUGHT ME, MOM

If I were forced to identify one dish that summed up all of my mom's cooking, it would have to be zucchini pancakes.

Born both out of creativity and desperation, they would appear late each summer. After weeks of eating zucchini— steamed and baked, breaded and fried— exhaustion set in. With the din of dinner complaints rising, Mom found an exciting new way to put zucchini on the table. And could a recipe be any cooler?

As anyone who has eaten zucchini bread knows, the vegetable works

equally well served sweet or savory. We would joyfully sit down to a plateful of these pancakes, dripping in real maple syrup. They were practical, delicious, inventive and comforting.

Stepping way out of her late-'70s comfort zone, she created a family classic. That's what you taught me in the kitchen, Mom. That's what I carry with me today.

I've tweaked the recipe a bit over the years. Bisquick gave way to potato starch. Fresh basil—and tarragon, when I have it—replace parsley. The ratio of zucchini to batter is much higher. I've even gussied up the name and call them "fritters." These days I usually serve them with a yogurt sauce, bright and fresh with mint, and smoky from paprika or cayenne. But I have to admit, maple syrup is still my favorite.

Tip: Resist the urge to squeeze the life out of the zucchini. Without a little remaining moisture the fritters can be dry. If your batter is too thick, add a tablespoon or two of cream or water.

mom's zucchini fritters

Serves 6-8 as a first plate or side
Heavy on fresh zucchini and bound gently with potato starch, these fritters are all about showcasing summer's (over) abundance. Low heat delivers a delicately crisp crust with a creamy interior.

For fritters:
4 cups grated zucchini, about 2 medium sized
1 egg, lightly beaten
2 tbs finely chopped, fresh basil
2 cloves garlic, minced
1 cup freshly grated Parmesan cheese
1/4 tsp Spanish paprika or cayenne pepper
1/4 cup potato starch or biscuit mix
Cream, as needed
4 tbs olive oil

For sauce:
1/2 cup whole yogurt, plain
2 tbs chopped, fresh mint
Paprika or cayenne

Directions:

- Place grated zucchini in colander over a bowl, sprinkle with 1 tsp salt. Let stand for 15-20 minutes then squeeze water from zucchini using your hands, or a tea towel.

- Make the sauce: Mix together the yogurt, mint. Add paprika or cayenne to taste.

- In a large bowl mix beaten egg, basil, garlic, Parmesan, paprika or cayenne, and potato starch. Add zucchini. Season lightly with salt and pepper.

- In a large skillet set over medium low heat, cook one small fritter in a little olive oil to check seasoning. Adjust with additional salt and pepper, fresh basil and cheese, as needed.

- Heat two tablespoons of olive oil in the skillet. Using 2-3 tablespoons of batter per fritter, cook them in batches adding additional oil as needed.

- Keep fritters hot in a warm oven while you finishing cooking all of the batter.

- Serve fritters topped with a dollop of the yogurt sauce.

GETTING IT JUST RIGHT

The batter should be slightly thicker than breakfast pancakes. If the batter is too dry, stir for a minute, which will release water from the zucchini. Add a tablespoon or two of cream as needed.

JONATHAN BARDZIK

Tip: The "count" for shrimp refers to the number of shrimp
in a pound. The higher the number, the smaller the shrimp.

Tip: Soak wooden skewers in water for an hour before loading
them up for the grill. This keeps them from burning.

grilled shrimp with peach and tarragon salsa

Serves 6

Tarragon, cucumber and red onion keep this salsa light and refreshing. It rocks here with grilled shrimp and is delicious over fish baked in foil or grilled chicken—use bone-in thighs for richer flavor. There will be enough left over from this recipe to enjoy the next day with a small bowl of tortilla chips.

For salsa:

1 large, firm tomato, seeded and diced

1 peach, peeled and diced

1/2 jalapeño, seeds & ribs removed, diced

1/2 red onion, diced

1/2 cucumber, peeled, seeded and diced

1/2 tsp sherry vinegar

1 tbs freshly squeezed lime juice

1 tbs minced tarragon

Pinch of cumin

Honey

For shrimp:

1 1/2 pounds 26-30 count shrimp

2 tbs olive oil

Directions:

- Mix together salsa ingredients in a large bowl. Put salsa in the refrigerator for at least 20 minutes allowing flavors to develop. Before serving, season to taste with a pinch of salt, pepper, and additional cumin as desired. The salsa can be made a day ahead.

- If the peach flavor isn't strong enough, add a little honey. The natural sugars bring the fruit forward again.

- Toss shrimp with oil and season lightly with salt and pepper. Skewer, piercing each shrimp twice so they don't spin on the skewer.

- Place over a medium grill and cook 2-3 minutes per side. They are ready when the shrimp turn opaque. Be careful not to overcook, which will make them dry.

PUTTING IT TOGETHER:

Arriving at the beach

It's the first weekend at your summer place. Raucous parties will follow in the days and nights ahead, but this evening's dinner is a deep sigh to celebrate the start of lazy summer days surrounded by good friends.

» Mom's Zucchini Fritters

» Grilled Shrimp with Peach Tarragon Salsa

» Corn-on-the-cob with Cilantro, Lime, Cumin Compound Butter

JONATHAN BARDZIK

Tip: Taste your berries.
If they are sweet,
use a sharper
balsamic. If they
are more acidic,
use your best sugary,
syrupy, aged vinegar.

blueberry balsamic spinach salad

Serves 6-8

This is the perfect opportunity to use your best olive oil and bust out those fruit-infused balsamic vinegars you get as gifts. Don't know what to do with strawberry or blackberry balsamic? Use it here.

For dressing:

1 shallot, minced
1/4 cup balsamic vinegar
1/2 tsp honey
1/4 tsp smoked sea salt
1/2 cup olive oil—use the good stuff!

For salad:

6-8 cups loose, fresh baby spinach leaves, about 1 pound
1 cup fresh blueberries

Directions:

- Whisk together shallot, vinegar, 1/4 tsp smoked salt and a pinch of pepper. Let rest for 5-10 minutes for flavors to develop.

- Pour the oil into the vinegar in a thin stream, while whisking. This will form a creamy emulsion.

- Taste the dressing with a spinach leaf. Season to taste with additional salt and pepper. Adjust the balance of oil and vinegar as needed.

- Toss together blueberries and spinach.

- Dress lightly. You've got good, farm-fresh spinach and blueberries and you want to taste them. (You may have dressing left over.)

UNUSUAL INGREDIENTS

"Darn it! I really wanted to make that recipe tonight but I don't have any whisky-plum jam." No one's pantry has everything. Go ahead and make a substitution.

Some are obvious. No smoked sea salt? Just use regular. But whisky-plum jam? Stop and think about flavors. The whisky is going to give it a bite, and plums are always more acidic than strawberries and blueberries. So use whatever jam you have. Just add a splash of whiskey and some lemon juice to reduce the sweetness.

And relax. This is supposed to be fun.

JONATHAN BARDZIK

25

THE REAL SECRET TO A QUICK, FABULOUS WEEKNIGHT DINNER.

It's 5:00 pm, and today has been long. The last thing I want to do is go home and cook, at least, not until I've opened a bottle of wine, which usually leads to an hour of sitting on the couch followed by dialing for dinner.

I've got a fridge filled with ripe tomatoes, sugary-sweet peaches, sockeye salmon and crisp green beans. Honestly, I would rather debate the Red Sox versus the Yankees (Sox, of course) than face another night of steamed veggies and baked fish.

I've just killed your buzz. You're thinking I arrive home each night with a basket of farm fresh produce on my arm to be carefully prepared, while discussing the events of the day with my loving husband, soothed by a soundtrack of classic jazz vocals. A long-stemmed glass of something fabulous in hand, we'll sit down to a candlelit evening at the dining room table, cloth napkins draped over our laps.

For real?! I've had a long day at the office, I'm beat and I want cheap Chinese and a bottle of cheap wine I won't taste after the second glass anyway. Which is when I think about compound butter.

Rolled in my fridge is a pound of farm-fresh, Amish butter. The other night I softened it and folded in fresh cilantro, lime zest, cumin and scallions. In under 30 minutes this evening I can sear a salmon filet, dress a salad and steam those green beans. A thin slice of the cilantro-lime butter will melt over the cooked fish. I'll toss another with the beans. Suddenly I face the prospect of a richly sauced, yet light, healthy dinner on the table.

Plus, it's cheaper than eating out, so we can treat ourselves to a better bottle. Something bubbly.

Tip: Once you roll the butter in
     parchment paper, twist the ends.
     This will form a neat, nearly
     perfect log.

cilantro lime cumin compound butter

Makes 16 one-tablespoon servings
Slices of the compound butter can be melted over fresh corn-on-the-cob, grilled meats or hearty fish like tuna or salmon. Try tossing a tablespoon with steamed green beans or zucchini.

Ingredients:

1/2 pound softened butter
1 tsp cumin
1/2 tsp chili powder or Spanish paprika
1 tsp finely grated lime zest
1/4 tsp white balsamic or champagne vinegar
2 scallions, whites plus 1 inch greens, finely minced
3 tbs finely chopped cilantro

Directions:

- Soften the butter at room temperature. Stir briefly in a medium bowl until creamy.
- With a rubber spatula, fold in the dry spices and lime zest.
- Fold in the vinegar a few drops at a time.
- Fold in the scallions and cilantro.
- Season to taste with salt and pepper.
- Using a piece of parchment paper or plastic wrap, roll the butter into a log and refrigerate until firm.

HAVE FUN. BE CREATIVE.

You can mix just about anything to make a compound butter. Here are a few combinations to get you started.

Basil, garlic and Parmesan: A classic. Mash garlic into a paste with salt, mince basil and add red wine vinegar. Finely grate Parmesan.

Cinnamon, honey and cayenne: Just the right sweet kick for corn on the cob, grilled chicken breasts, and fresh biscuits.

Tarragon, scallion and white wine vinegar: Light and delicate. Perfect for grilled halibut or foil baked white fish. Toss it with steamed green beans or over heirloom tomatoes.

Lemon, garlic and parsley: It's classic Gremolata in a butter. Mash garlic into a paste with salt. Add finely grated lemon zest and minced parsley with a few drops of champagne vinegar.

JONATHAN BARDZIK

Tip: Worried the jalapeño is too hot? Most of the heat is in the seeds and ribs you remove. You can always use less (or more!).

corn and zucchini orzo

Serves 6-8 as a side

Light, sweet flavors of summer are made bright with a splash of vinegar and the zing of jalapeño. This tastes just as good hot as it does as a cold pasta salad. This is also wonderfully light made with fresh egg pasta.

Ingredients:

2 tbs olive oil

1 large yellow onion, diced

3 cloves of garlic, minced

1/2 jalapeño, seeds and ribs removed, minced

2 cups finely diced zucchini, about 1-2 medium

2 ears corn, kernels removed

1 cup orzo, uncooked

2 tbs butter

2-3 tbs chopped cilantro or parsley

Sherry vinegar

Directions:

- Bring 4 quarts of water to a boil in a large pot. Salt heavily—about 2 tbs.

- Heat olive oil in a 12" sauté pan over medium heat. Add onion and cook until softened.

- Add garlic and jalapeño and cook another 30 seconds until fragrant.

- Turn up heat to medium high and add zucchini.

- When you add the zucchini to the pan, add the orzo to the pot of boiling water.

- When zucchini is tender but still firm in the center, add corn and cook 1 minute longer, about the time the orzo is ready.

- When pasta is still undercooked, just shy of al dente, just a little too firm in the center, strain it, reserving 1 cup cooking liquid. Add orzo and liquid to vegetables. Cook until water has evaporated.

- Add cilantro and butter. Season to taste with vinegar, salt and pepper.

GETTING IT JUST RIGHT

I like to cut the zucchini down to the same size as the corn kernels to balance the flavors. You can save yourself some knife work and cut smaller zucchinis into half circles. Tossing small ingredients with large pasta results in all the vegetables settling to the bottom of the bowl. By using small pasta, like orzo, they blend together. Don't skip the butter. It's less than 1/8th tbs per serving, and gives the dish wonderful, sweet richness.

JONATHAN BARDZIK

IS YOUR BREAD TOO BIG?

With the exception of Jesus, no one ever seems plagued by having too little bread. (And he resolved that issue handily!)

Just look at the myriad recipes created expressly to use up leftover loaves: crostini and croutons, bread pudding and bread crumbs. With all due deference to good bread and skilled bakers, are we simply making our loaves of bread too big?

The simple answer is "no." Leftover bread is a gift, its value no more apparent than in Panzanella, an Italian salad of stale croutons and tomatoes. The salad is dressed with sharp vinegar and olive oil to soften the bread. Paired with garden fresh tomatoes, the salad is light, not heavy.

You don't even have to wait for the bread to get stale. Grab a fresh, toothy, crusty, country loaf and toast cubes in a little olive oil. You may never have leftover bread again.

Tip: The bread will get soggy over time, so add
the bread and dress right before serving.
To make enough for leftovers, store the
vegetables, bread and dressing separately.

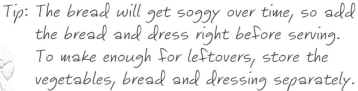

Tip: Tart, early-season tomatoes will taste better with
more oil in the dressing. Sweet summer tomatoes will
handle a higher proportion of acidic vinegar.

tomato panzanella

Serves 8

This is a wonderful way to use up the other half of that beautiful baguette or loaf of sourdough you brought home from the farm market. Make sure the bread has toasted through, or is stale and hard, so it holds up to the dressing without turning to mush.

For salad:
- 6 cups fresh country bread cut in 1" pieces
- 1/4 cup olive oil
- 3 large, perfect tomatoes, cut into 1" pieces, about 4 cups (My favorites are the heirlooms Brandywine and Black Cherokee.)
- 1 red onion, halved and thinly sliced
- 1/4 cup thinly sliced basil

For dressing:
- 2 cloves garlic
- 1/2 tsp mustard
- 1/3 cup red wine vinegar
- 2/3 cups olive oil— the good stuff!

Directions:

- Toss bread in 1/4 cup olive oil, salt and pepper.

- Toast bread in a 400 degree oven or a sauté pan over medium heat until golden brown and crisp. About 5-7 minutes.

- Toss together tomatoes, onion and basil.

- Make dressing: Pound garlic with a pinch of coarse sea salt into a paste. Whisk together garlic paste, mustard, vinegar and black pepper. Pour the oil into the vinegar in a thin stream, while whisking. This will form a creamy emulsion.

- Check the flavor of the dressing with a piece of tomato. Season to taste with additional, salt, pepper, oil or vinegar.

- Add bread to the tomatoes and toss through with the dressing.

PUTTING IT TOGETHER:

A vegetarian birthday party

Meat eaters won't complain with hearty pasta and crispy toasted bread on the menu. Serve the pasta cold and you can make everything ahead of time. Just dress the salads at the last minute so your greens and croutons don't get soggy.

» Blueberry Balsamic Spinach Salad

» Corn and Zucchini Orzo

» Tomato Panzanella

JONATHAN BARDZIK

party!

bold flavors for bright summer days

WHEN A PARTY COMES KNOCKING.

"Don't worry about my birthday," I halfheartedly told my husband, Jason. Between work travel, weekly cooking demonstrations at Eastern Market and still trying to finish unpacking in our new home, planning a party felt like too much work.

Two days after my birthday (it's in August, just in case you want to send a card) we met at our Metro station to walk home together. Swinging into the grocery store, Jason encouraged me to pick up some chips, salsa and frozen pizza rolls. "No, I'm trying to be good," I said, thinking about the farm-fresh vegetables in our fridge. I conceded a few bottles of wine.

Arriving home I resisted the siren song of the couch and hit the kitchen, grabbing a few tortillas, some cheese and some beautiful, ripe tomatoes for quesadillas. About to put the first one in the pan, I heard a knock at the door. "Go answer it," Jason said.

Opening the door, I discovered our friends Mark and Seth. "Happy birthday!" they boomed. "We stopped

by to drop off your gift." A little odd,
I thought, but sweet. We walked into
the kitchen, Jason grabbed four glasses
and poured wine. I started cooking the
quesadilla. Knock, knock.

I answered the door again, welcoming
in Ed and John. Still addled from a
hectic day, I was confused. The picture,
however, came into clear focus over
the next 15 minutes as 20 more friends
arrived bearing bottles of wine and cards.

Seemingly with fishes and loaves, there
was enough food for everyone. Bold and
bright summer flavors—tomatoes, basil,
peaches (and a little bacon)—made the
cooking simple. It was a party, boisterous
and warm. And it was exactly what I
needed.

Summer parties are simple and fun.
Bright pots growing with flowers and
a few strands of lights make things
festive. If you don't have time to plan
and decorate, nothing says "party!"
like frozen fruit and rum whirring in a
blender while you light up the grill. The
guest list? The more the merrier!

WHAT TO DRINK: AND BE MERRY

Beer—Leave heavy beers behind and grab
   something lighter with your grilled steaks
   and shrimp (or a good ol' fashioned burger!).
   Steam Beer—technically a lager—drinks
   like a light ale. A perfect choice! Or follow
   the Germans' lead—it is beer after all—and
   grab a Hefeweizen/Witbier style brew.
   Easily drinkable with good body, pick up
   a few six-packs and find your favorite!

Wine—When it comes to party wine for a large
   group of friends take a cue from the Spanish.
   Sangria isn't just delicious and easy to drink,
   but was designed to deliver an economic
   and satisfying buzz to a crowd. The basic
   recipe? Equal amounts lemon, lime or orange
   soda and wine, a tablespoon of sugar to
   sweeten, a shot or two of brandy to fortify
   and lots of chopped fruit. Experiment with
   different wines, fruits, sodas and liquors
   to give every party a signature cocktail.

Cocktails—Whether it's happy hour or a party
   by the pool, summer's more fun when the
   drinks are fruity and frozen. Freeze fresh
   berries, peaches and plums, blend them with
   vodka or rum and add a tablespoon or two
   of simple syrup—that's 1 cup sugar and 1
   cup water—infused with fresh herbs like
   chocolate mint, Thai basil and lemon verbena.

MUSIC: PARTY TIME!

It's a summer play list of feel-good songs whether you want to rock out at the grill or party on in the pool.

New Order—*Blue Monday*
The Rosebuds—*You Better Get Ready*
B-52's—*Rock Lobster*
Mark Ronson & the Business—*Bang Bang Bang*
Zac Brown Band—*Jump Right In*
Amy Ray—*Let it Ring*
Dave Matthews—*Ants Marching*
Panic at the Disco—*Nine in the Afternoon*
Hot Chip—*One Pure Thought*
Vampire Weekend—*Walcott*
Scissor Sisters—*San Louis Obispo*
Pizzicato Five—*Happy Sad*

JONATHAN BARDZIK

41

Tip: Nothing slices quesadillas better than a pizza cutter. Cutting them with a knife always pushes the ingredients out the sides.

Tip: You can find Chinese five-spice powder in the spice section at most grocery stores.

peach quesadillas

Serves 5 as a main dish or 10 as an appetizer

Sugary summer peaches are a bold balance for rich pork sausage and bright cumin, Chinese five-spice powder and a splash of soy. These quesadillas are an instant summer party!

Ingredients:

6 tbs olive oil

3 large pork sausage links

1 tsp Chinese five-spice powder

1 tbs soy sauce

1 red onion, diced

1/4 tsp cumin

10 6" corn tortillas

2 1/2 cups grated Cheddar cheese

3 peaches, peeled and thinly sliced

1/4 cup chopped basil

Directions:

- Warm 1 tbs olive oil in a 10" skillet over medium-high heat. Remove the sausage from the casings and add to pan with Chinese five-spice powder and soy sauce.

- Breaking up the sausage as it cooks, sauté until browned and cooked through.

- Remove sausage from pan with a slotted spoon and set aside.

- Add onion to pan and sauté until softened and edges begin to brown. If pan is dry, add 1 tbs olive oil.

- Stir in cumin and season to taste with salt and pepper.

- To assemble quesadillas, layer one corn tortilla with 1/4 cup cheese, cooked sausage, peach slices, onions and basil. Top with another 1/4 cup cheese and a second tortilla. Repeat with remaining ingredients to make 5 quesadillas.

- Fry each quesadillas in 1 tbs oil over medium heat, about 3 minutes per side, turning once when the tortilla begins to brown in spots. With a pizza cutter, slice into wedges and serve.

PUTTING IT TOGETHER:

Pool party!

Whether diving into the deep end or chilling your feet in the kiddie pool, turn on the happy tunes, bring out bold, easy snacks and laze the afternoon away, cocktail in hand. Cannonball!

» Peach Quesadillas

» Asian Peanut Noodle Salad

» Watermelon Martini

JONATHAN BARDZIK

43

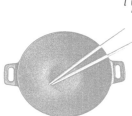

Tip: When stir frying you don't want to crowd the pan. Cooking ingredients in separate batches and combining them at the end keeps your pan hot so your ingredients brown rather than braising in a pool of water.

stir-fried thai eggplant

Serves 6–8

I constantly crave Asian take-out. This is even better! Using fresh ingredients to make it from scratch means less salt, no corn syrup and lots of bold, bright flavor. If you can't find long, thin Japanese eggplant, use the familiar, dark-purple Italian ones.

Ingredients:

- 4 tbs peanut oil
- 4 cups Japanese or Italian eggplant cut in 1 1/2" cubes
- 2 cups thinly sliced Shitake mushrooms
- 1 medium red pepper, thinly sliced
- 1 clove garlic, minced
- 1/2 cup Thai or common, Italian basil, loosely packed

Sauce:

- 2 tbs soy sauce
- 2 tbs palm sugar or brown sugar
- 1 tbs fish sauce
- 1 tbs sesame or hot chile oil
- 1 tbs rice wine vinegar
- 1 tbs cornstarch
- 1/4 cup warm water

Directions:

- Whisk together the sauce ingredients in a small bowl. Set aside.

- Heat 2 tbs peanut oil in a large skillet over medium-high heat. Add eggplant and cook approximately 5 minutes until softened and golden. The eggplant will look translucent. Remove from skillet.

- Reduce heat to medium, add remaining 1 tbs peanut oil to same skillet. Add red pepper and Shitake mushrooms.

- Cook 3-5 minutes until softened. Add to reserved, cooked eggplant.

- In the empty skillet, heat 1 tbs peanut oil. Add garlic and cook 1 minute until fragrant. Return vegetables to pan and warm through, about 2 minutes.

- Re-whisk sauce and add to vegetables. Simmer, stirring occasionally, until liquid is reduced and coats the vegetables.

- Add basil and stir through. Season to taste with white or black pepper.

FISH SAUCE? PALM SUGAR?

For those of us not lucky enough to live near ethnic specialty markets, most grocery stores have good international aisles. Worried that you'll never use ingredients like fish sauce and palm sugar again? You can adapt this recipe all season long using everything from spring asparagus to roasted cubes of winter squash. The quality of fish sauce varies widely. If there's a more expensive bottle, it's well worth the investment, likely to be no more than an additional $1-2.

JONATHAN BARDZIK

45

Tip: Craft cocktails take a little extra effort, but choosing one special
   drink for an evening turns a simple get together into a party!
   Prepare the ingredients ahead of time and mix them to order.

DC Public Library

Author: Bardzik, Jonathan,
Title: Simple summer : a recipe
for cooking and entertai
Item ID: 31172077271716
Date charged: 3/17/2022,17:28
Date due: 4/7/2022,23:59

Thank you for using the
DC Public Library

watermelon martini

Serves 4

Sweet and light with the exotic spice of Thai basil and fresh juniper berry note of smooth gin, this cocktail is an easy drink. Maybe too easy! If you want to lighten it up, add a splash of club soda.

Ingredients:

1 1/2 cups fresh pressed watermelon juice—recipe below
1/2 cup smooth gin
1/2 cup Thai basil simple syrup—recipe below
2 tablespoon Ruby Red Grapefruit or other bitters
Lime slice to garnish

Directions:

- In a cocktail shaker with ice, add watermelon juice, gin, simple syrup and bitters.

- Shake and strain into a martini or lowball glass with ice. Garnish with a lime slice.

- Squeeze the lime slice into cocktail right before drinking.

Watermelon juice:

To make watermelon juice, press cubed watermelon through a food mill or purée in a food processor. Strain the juice through a sieve and then again through a sieve lined with cheese cloth.

Thai basil syrup:

Stir together 1/2 cup sugar and 1/2 cup water over medium-high heat. Simmer until the sugar dissolves. Remove from heat, and add 1 loosely packed cup whole basil leaves. Let steep for 15-20 minutes and strain to remove solids.

YOUR SIGNATURE DRINK

My husband Jason doesn't like gin, so we make his with vodka. My friend Nancy, makes the simple syrup with mint, uses rum and a splash of soda, and turns this recipe into a Mojito. My friend Sam left out the alcohol altogether and made it sparkle with seltzer and an extra splash of lime. You're the bartender and it's your party. Make it your own.

JONATHAN BARDZIK

VEGETABLES AREN'T CANDY

You know when parents talk about sneaking vegetables into their kids' food? None of us really believe that it works, right? Vegetable strips are not "French fries," shredded vegetable patties aren't "burgers," and raisins may be sweet, but nature's candy is a bridge too far.

Zucchini, however, is a different animal altogether. Put it in cookies, pancakes, bread and pizza, and I'll gladly be fooled any day of the week. It was my Mom's recipe for zucchini pizza—where shredded zucchini mixed with a little cheese, flour and egg forms the crust—that inspired this meatloaf.

It does everything that "sneaking-in-veggies" recipes are supposed to. It turns a pound of ground beef into eight, hearty servings, each of which has almost half a cup of zucchini. Replacing the usual tomato paste with a homemade tomato jam sneaks half a tomato in there too, along with an amazing amount of flavor. All these veggies leave you, and your meatloaf, feeling light and summery.

Tip: Salt-cured, Italian Pancetta lends this meatloaf a lighter flavor than smoky bacon. If you want to remove some of that smoky flavor from bacon, simmer it in water for a couple minutes before dicing it.

zucchini meatloaf

Serves 8

Lightened with shredded zucchini, this meatloaf has a nice summer weight. Making a quick tomato jam lends sweeter, fresher taste than ketchup or tomato paste.

Ingredients:

1/4 pound pancetta or bacon, diced

1 medium onion, diced

2 cloves garlic, minced

4 tomatoes, seeded and diced

1/4 cup Sherry vinegar

2 medium or 4 small zucchini
    shredded, about 3 1/2 cups

1 pound ground beef,—
    ask for 80% lean

1 cup Panko bread crumbs

2 eggs, lightly beaten

2 tbs chopped basil

1 1/2 cups Parmesan cheese

Directions:

- In a large skillet, sauté pancetta or bacon and one tbs olive oil over medium heat, until crisp. Remove meat with a slotted spoon and reserve.

- Add onion. Cook until soft, about 5 minutes. Add garlic. Cook 1 minute until fragrant.

- Add tomato and cook until thick and jammy, about 10-12 minutes. Add a little water if pan gets dry before the tomatoes have fully broken down.

- Add vinegar to the pan with the tomato jam, and bring to a simmer, scraping up any brown bits from the bottom. Season to taste with salt and pepper.

- Mix the warm tomato jam in a bowl with the reserved pancetta, shredded zucchini, ground beef, Panko, eggs, basil and cheese. Season lightly with salt and pepper.

- Fry a small patty of the mixture, then season to taste adding additional salt, pepper, Parmesan cheese or vinegar as needed.

- Press into a 9" square baking dish. Place pan on a rimmed sheet pan—the meatloaf may bubble over—and bake at 325 degrees for about an hour.

- Tent with foil and let rest 10 minutes before serving.

WHAT IS PANKO?

Panko is a Japanese style of bread crumbs. You can find them in the international aisle or at the fish counter. Panko is crisp, sharp-edged and coarser than Italian bread crumbs. It is also unseasoned, which means a whole lot less salt. I use them for fried zucchini and over foil-baked fish. Toast a 1/2 cup of Panko in a skillet with 1 tbs of butter and a tbs or two of fresh herbs to dress up steamed vegetables when company is coming (or hoard all of this deliciousness for yourself!).

Tip: Removing kernels from ears of corn can be a messy
   process. Stop the kernel explosion by inverting a small
   bowl inside a large one. Stand the ear of corn on the
   small bowl and gently slice the kernels off the cob.

corn and bacon succotash

Serves 6-8

Using canned or frozen Lima beans seems criminal at the height of summer. Plentiful green beans keep this succotash light and farm fresh.

Ingredients:

3 slices thick bacon, diced

1 small onion, diced

2 cloves garlic

1 lb green beans, stem ends removed, cut into 3/4" pieces

1 red pepper, diced

3 ears of corn, kernels removed

1 tbs fresh, chopped thyme

1/4 tsp cayenne pepper

1 tbs butter

Sherry vinegar

Directions:

- Sauté bacon in a large skillet over medium heat until browned and cooked through.

- Remove with a slotted spoon and set aside.

- Add onion to skillet with bacon fat and cook until softened, about 5 minutes. Add garlic and cook 30 seconds until fragrant.

- Add green beans and pepper to pan and sauté for 5 minutes.

- Add corn, reduce heat to medium-low and cook, covered, for 10-15 minutes until vegetables softened but still crisp.

- Remove lid, add thyme and reserved bacon. Cook an additional 3 minutes.

- Add cayenne pepper and butter and stir through. Season to taste with salt, pepper and a splash of vinegar for brightness.

PUTTING IT TOGETHER:

Help! My garden just exploded!

You walk out to the garden on a July morning and your formerly small zucchini plant has tripled in size, seemingly overnight, and is now loaded with 15 giant squash. Not to mention the bushel of corn your Dad dropped on the front steps. Call your friends. It's time for a party!

» Ruby Plum Soup

» Zucchini Meatloaf

» Corn and Bacon Succotash

JONATHAN BARDZIK

Tip: Rule #1 of barbecue sauce: use it toward the end of cooking, about 2 minutes per side. Place brushed ingredients just to the side, not directly over, the hot coals, so they glaze rather than burning the sugars in the sauce.

Tip: How long will the remaining sauce store?
We have no idea. We keep eating all of ours.

pork chops with peach barbecue sauce

Serves 6

Barbecue sauce is about achieving the perfect balance of sugar and acidity.
Brush this sauce on grilled peaches to capture the sweet taste of midsummer.
(Ice cold beer helps, too.)

Ingredients:

2 tbs butter

1/2 medium red onion, diced, about 1 cup

2 peaches, diced

1 tbs minced ginger

1 cup molasses

1 cup ketchup

1/2 cup white vinegar

1/2 tsp cardamom

1/2 tsp chili powder

1/2 tsp dried mustard

1/2 tsp cumin

1/4 cup hot chili oil or chili sauce

6 thick-cut pork chops

Directions:

- In a small saucepan over medium-high heat, sauté onion in butter until softened.

- Add peaches and ginger. Cook until peaches are soft and can be easily mashed with a fork. If your pan gets dry add a little water to keep peaches from burning.

- Add all remaining ingredients except chili oil (and the pork chops!) and simmer for 20 minutes until thickened.

- Add chili oil or chile sauce and simmer for 2 additional minutes to bring ingredients together. Season to taste.

- Season pork chops with salt and pepper. Sear on a hot grill, about 3 minutes per side.

- Move off of direct heat and cook until nearly cooked through, about 130 degrees.

- Brush generously with barbecue sauce and turn pork. Cook two minutes over indirect heat, allowing sauce to cook to a glaze. Brush top with more sauce, turn and cook two minutes longer.

- Remove from grill, tent with foil and let rest for 10 minutes. Serve with more sauce.

GETTING IT JUST RIGHT

Barbecue sauce is the American answer to Asia's sweet and sour dishes. Vinegar and sugar are boldly balanced by rich, sweet meats like pork, chicken and shrimp. In this recipe, sugary molasses and peaches work with acidic ketchup and vinegar. The exotic (but readily available!) mix of spices adds depth and warmth while chili sauce adds just the right kick. Season to taste at the end, adding more molasses for sweet or vinegar for sour.

JONATHAN BARDZIK

TAKE A CHANCE ON ME

I love when a new recipe directs me to an ingredient I have never heard of or worked with before. There's that moment of fear at the market when you say the name out loud for the first time, wondering just how horribly you've botched its pronunciation.

There's the prickly anticipation when you first taste it, knowing you may have completely screwed up, rendering this special, new ingredient nearly inedible. Finally you serve it, smiling, to your dinner guests and tell them it's quite possibly the best thing you've ever tasted, hoping desperately that they've never heard of it before either.

This is cooking at it's best. I love nothing more than trying new ingredients or recipes—taking a chance, failing miserably sometimes, and getting right back on that figurative horse. After all, it's the only way you learn, and there is joy and fellowship in sharing these adventures with others.

So grab some soba noodles—Japanese buckwheat pasta—light, clean, Japanese tamari soy sauce, deep, roasted sesame oil and that odd beast—fresh, unsalted peanut butter with a skim of oil over the top—and make this wonderful cold summer salad. Feel free to get it wrong a few times, but each time you bring it to the table smile, tell them it's magnificent, and enjoy every minute of your time together.

Tip: I like the fresh taste of unsweeted peanut butter. You can find organic brands on your grocery store shelf. The oil separates and rises to the top. Just stir it into the jar before using. If you are allergic to peanuts, try Tahini, a toasted sesame seed paste which you can find in the international food aisle.

Tip: Tamari soy sauce, a lighter-tasting, Japanese-style soy has less of a sharp bite than its Chinese counterpart. It is also available wheat-free for gluten-free eaters.

asian peanut noodle salad

Serves 6

I love cold peanut noodles in the summer. The starchy pasta and rich peanut butter is hearty and filling while crisp cucumber, bright scallions and cilantro keep it cool and light for hot nights.

Ingredients:

  1/2 pound soba noodles

  1 large cucumber

  2 scallions, white and green parts, thinly sliced

  2 tbs toasted sesame seeds

  1/4 cup chopped cilantro

Dressing:

  1/4 cup fresh, unsalted peanut butter

  1/4 cup water

  3 tbs soy sauce

  2 tbs sesame oil

  1/4 cup rice wine vinegar

  Sriracha hot sauce

Directions:

- Cook noodles by adding to boiling, unsalted water. When al dente, drain and rinse with cold water.

- Peel the cucumber, slice it in half the long way and scrape out the seeds with a spoon. Cut into thin slices.

- Make the dressing: Thin the peanut butter by whisking it for a minute with 1/4 cup warm water.

- Whisk in soy sauce, sesame oil and rice wine vinegar. Add Sriracha to taste.

- Add dressing to noodles and toss. Start with 3/4 of the dressing and add more as needed.

- Serve topped with cucumbers, scallions, fresh cilantro and sesame seeds.

TO RINSE OR NOT TO RINSE?

It's a subject of endless debate. Some Italian purists purchase pairs of pince-nez just so they can look down their Roman noses at those who dare to rinse the flavorful starches from freshly boiled pasta. While I agree that Italian pasta is best sauced without a wash, Asian pastas call for different treatment. Whether cooking rice sticks for Pad Thai or soba noodles for this salad, Asia's chefs give them a cleansing rinse. You should, too.

JONATHAN BARDZIK

Tip: No buttermilk? Blend 1 cup of whole milk or cream with 1 tbs lemon juice or white vinegar and let sit for 5 minutes.

ruby plum soup

Serves 6-8 as a first course

I love cold fruit soups, but don't want them to taste like dessert. Buttermilk and red wine give sugary plums enough balance to start a savory, summer supper. This is served cold, so prepare well ahead of time.

Ingredients:

6 plums, pitted and diced

1 tbs finely minced, fresh ginger

1 cup dry red wine (like Cabernet Sauvignon)

2 tbs honey

1 cup buttermilk

1/4 cup white balsamic vinegar

Directions:

- Place plums in a saucepan and cook over medium heat for five minutes.

- Add wine. Cover and cook for five minutes more.

- Remove from stove and let cool to room temperature.

- Pass half the cooked plums through a food mill or processor. Add to a bowl with the remaining stewed plums and stir together.

- Stir in honey and buttermilk.

- Season to taste with vinegar. Add half of of the vinegar at first and add more as needed. The amount you use depends on how sugary your plums are.

- Chill soup until cold—about 30 minutes—before serving. Soup can be made a day ahead.

PUTTING IT TOGETHER:

Saturday night at the lake

Whether you've aggressively tackled mountain biking, kayaking or a really thin, trashy, summer read, Saturday night is time to crank some tunes, fill a tall glass with something cold and enjoy the good friends and family who've joined you for this weekend escape.

» Grilled Pork Chops with Peach Barbecue Sauce

» Stir-fried Thai Eggplant

» Asian Peanut Noodle Salad

JONATHAN BARDZIK

too darn hot:

cool cooking for summer's dog days

WHAT DID YOU HAVE FOR DINNER ON JULY 4TH 1999?

My husband, Jason, will tell you that I can't remember what I was talking about ten minutes ago, but I can tell you exactly what I had for dinner on the third Tuesday of June, 15 years ago. I'm not quite that good, but I do have a memory for meals.

Many of those memories come from summer. Long, late, lazy meals with family and friends: fresh fish with the Creelmans in Madaket on Nantucket, lobsters and cornbread with the Bugbees on Southport Island, ME, my first frogs legs on Bastille Day at the beach in Newport, RI.

I remember on the Fourth of July 1998 making the same baked beans and ham that Gram Forgiel made for my Mom as a child. Fourth of July 1999 was a honeydew and cantaloupe salad with ginger and honey, and grilled lamb chops, served cold from the night before, with a tequila, lime, kiwi chutney cooked quickly in the microwave to keep the colors bright and the kitchen cool.

Summer meals are memorable because they don't compete. There's no thirty-day panic and planning like we have for big winter holidays. The meals are not grand nor the expectations high. The food is fresh, the techniques simple, and the flavors are as bright as our memories of them.

WHAT TO DRINK: GRAB A COLD ONE

Beer—Heavy beer fills you up, leaving no room for eating. If only the Germans had come up with a solution...oh right, they did. Kolcsh is perfect on a hot summer day. Every brewer does it a little differently, but they're always good. Or grab an old-fashioned Pilsner. Light and crisp, it's a lawnmower brew for real beer drinkers. If you really want to impress your friends (and treat yourself) grab a Saison. Traditionally brewed by farmers in winter for drinking in summer, its spiced flavors pair perfectly with grilled meats and bright fruits.

Wine—Keep it crisp. Spanish Albariño, acidic and peachy. Floral Viognier and German Gewürztraminer, with the flavor of lychee. Sweeter bottles will win over the most diehard White Zinfandel devotees, while drier bottles will satisfy Sauvignon Blanc fans on the sultriest summer afternoon. With Gewürztraminer look for the word "trocken" (dry).

Cocktails—Alcohol-free family fun doesn't relegate your cocktail menu to powder-based punch. Blend fresh-pressed fruit juices like watermelon, peach and cantaloupe with a splash of sparkling seltzer. Crush tart blackberries, mint and a pinch of sugar in the bottom of each glass. You can always add rum or Champagne after the kids go to bed.

MUSIC: LANGUID AND LAZY

This is the perfect soundtrack for sultry afternoons spent hanging in the shade or family dinners on the screened in porch. It's summer music, fun and free, easy and smooth.

Mat Kearney—*Hey Mama*
Belle and Sebastian—*Funny Little Frog*
Air—*Cherry Blossom Girl*
Jack Johnson—*Upside Down*
Roxy Music—*Avalon*
The Shins—*Phantom Limb*
The Whiffenpoofs—*Too Darn Hot*
Modest Mouse—*Missed the Boat*
k.d.lang—*Suddenly*
Chris Isaak—*Two Hearts*
Ibrahim Ferrer—*Boquinene*
George Michael—*Please Send Me Someone*

Tip: I love meaty, heirloom tomatoes in this soup.
Try Black Cherokee or Brandywine—with
perfectly balanced sweet, acidic flavor.

Tip: How do you pick a ripe watermelon? Sniff? Thump? Weight is
a good indicator of a watermelon that is fresh and juicy.
My method? I just ask the farmers at the market. With dozens
of watermelons passing through their hands each day, they're the experts.

watermelon gazpacho

Serves 6-8
Salt brings out the tomato, and honey makes the watermelon pop.
Leave out the watermelon juice, add some cumin and serve this as a
salsa over fried fish tacos!

Ingredients:

   6 cups watermelon diced and separated

   2 large tomatoes, diced, about 2 cups

   1/2 red onion, diced

   1/2 tsp lime zest

   2 tbs lime juice

   1/2 jalapeño, seeded and minced

   2 tbs basil, finely chopped

   1/4 cup red wine vinegar

   2 tbs honey

Directions:

- Mix together 4 cups of the diced watermelon with the tomato and onion.

- Add lime zest and juice, jalapeño and basil. Stir together.

- Press remaining 2 cups of watermelon through a food mill or purée in a food processor and strain through a fine sieve to remove solids.

- Add watermelon juice, vinegar and honey to soup. Season to taste with salt, pepper and additional honey, if needed.

- If you make this soup ahead of time, check the seasoning again before serving. The watermelon and tomatoes will release more moisture and dilute the salt, vinegar and honey.

WHEN WATERMELON GOES MISSING

Tomatoes and watermelon have become a popular pairing. Developing this recipe, I mixed bright, fresh heirloom tomatoes with sweet, crisp watermelon. A pinch of salt made the tomato flavor robust, but the watermelon was weak, barely there.

Where salt heightens savory flavors, sugar highlights sweet ingredients. A drizzle of honey brought back the sweet watermelon. Fresh basil gave life and depth. A splash of bright vinegar brought it all together. Season to taste!

JONATHAN BARDZIK

HIGH AS AN ELEPHANT'S EYE

My Dad did his PhD thesis on corn. At night my Mom typed out page after page, over 100, on a typewriter. Corn expertise was highly regarded in our home. Dad taught us that all vegetables have sugars, which once harvested, convert to starch. This happens faster in some vegetables than others. Corn is one of the fastest.

Growing up, when corn was on the dinner menu, Dad and I would stop by Sapowsky's and wait in their dirt driveway in front of the farm stand. When the next tractor pulled up with a cart of freshly picked corn, Dad would grab a dozen ears and head home, where Mom already had water boiling. As soon as we pulled into the driveway I would get out and shuck the corn, which Mom would boil for a couple of minutes. We would eat it, hot and fresh, usually without any wholly unnecessary butter and salt.

Today's cultivars of corn have more stable sugars, but corn is still best picked during the cool hours of the morning, quickly refrigerated and eaten as soon as possible.

Tip: Garlic and salt mashed together into a
   paste will more evenly distribute through your
   dressing, meaning no big, sharp chunks!

herbed goat cheese raw corn salad

Serves 6

This is a perfect, light summer picnic salad. Serve it alongside herb and wine poached chicken and a perfect loaf of crusty country bread slathered in farm-fresh butter. Just a thought.

Ingredients:
- 4 ears corn
- 1 red onion, diced

For dressing:
- 1 clove garlic, minced
- 2 tbs mild goat cheese
- 1 tbs finely chopped tarragon
- 1 tbs lemon juice
- 1/4 cup white balsamic vinegar
- 1/2 cup olive oil—the good stuff!

Directions:
- Slice kernels from the corn. Toss with onion in a medium bowl.
- Mash garlic into a paste with coarse salt by dragging it across your cutting board with the flat side of your knife.
- Stir together garlic paste, cheese, tarragon, lemon juice and vinegar.
- Pour the oil into the dressing in a thin stream, while whisking. This will form a creamy emulsion.
- Lightly dress corn and onions.

PUTTING IT TOGETHER:
Concert on the lawn

Spread a blanket, unpack your picnic basket and watch the fireflies dance as the band warms up. It's a hot night, but your cold-packed meal, and a tall pitcher of sun tea will cool things down.

» French Potato and Tomato Salad

» Herbed Corn and Goat Cheese Salad

» White Wine and Herb Poached Chicken

JONATHAN BARDZIK

Tip: The clean citrus flavor from the zest of fruits like lemons, limes and oranges comes just from the colorful skin. The white pith underneath is bitter. Run each side of the lime just once or twice over a grater.

Tip: Habañero chile powder is sweet and fruity, not smoky. It also delivers a lot of heat—a little will go a long way. Avoid measuring a "pinch" with your fingers—use the tip of a spoon—so you don't have to worry about rubbing your eyes later.

cantaloupe peach nectarine salsa

Makes 4 cups salsa

Sweet summer fruit gets a bright pop from lime zest and a finish of heat from ground habañero chili powder. Serve it over last night's smoky, grilled chicken, straight from the fridge, or just eat it right out of the bowl!

Ingredients:

1 cup diced white nectarine, about 2
1 cup diced white peach, about 2
2 cups diced cantaloupe
1/2 tsp cardamom
Pinch Habañero or other chili powder
1/2 tsp grated lime zest
2 tbs honey
1 tbs white balsamic vinegar
1/2 cup yogurt
1 tbs lime juice

Directions:

- Mix together nectarine, peach and cantaloupe in a medium bowl.
- Stir in cardamom, habañero, lime zest, 1 tbs honey, vinegar and a pinch of salt. Chill for 20 minutes to let flavors blend.
- Mix together yogurt, remaining 1 tbs honey and lime juice.
- Stir chilled salsa to coat with juices and serve with yogurt "sour cream."

SOME LIKE IT HOT!

Not all chilies are created equal. Some, like the jalapeño, will get you pleasantly fired up, while others, like habañeros and Scotch Bonnets, may really burn. If you are unfamiliar, go slowly. Do a little reading and remember that, in this case, safe is definitely better than sorry.

However you like your heat, remember to keep it in your mouth. Either wear gloves or wash your hands several times after cutting these incendiary peppers. The chemical that gives them their heat, capsaicin, is the same chemical found in a can of pepper spray. Sometimes you can even feel a mild burn from just wiping the sweat from your brown on a hot summer day.

Tip: Keep fresh herbs like basil, tarragon and mint in a glass or vase like fresh flowers. They stay fresh, are easily within reach and look beautiful.

white wine and herb poached chicken

Serves 6

I love poached chicken served cold. It is perfectly moist. The dry wine, peppercorns and bay ground a beautiful sauce made slightly sweet by the chicken, tarragon and butter.

Ingredients:

2 tbs olive oil

1 onion, diced

2 cloves garlic, minced

6 chicken breast halves

3 sprigs tarragon

3-4 sprigs parsley

4-5 chives

2 cups dry white wine

2 cups chicken or vegetable stock

1/2 tsp whole peppercorns

2 bay leaves

2 tbs white wine vinegar

2 tbs cold butter, cut in pieces

Directions:

- Warm oil over medium heat in a large skillet. Add onion and sauté until softened and translucent, about 6-7 minutes. Reduce heat if needed, to cook onions without browning.

- Add garlic and cook two minutes, until fragrant.

- Place chicken breasts in pan in a single layer. Tuck herbs between chicken.

- Mix together wine and stock, and pour into pan.

- Cover pan and bring to a simmer. Cook chicken for 10-15 minutes until done, 165 degrees. Be careful not to let poaching liquid boil.

- Remove chicken to a platter and tent with foil.

- Add peppercorns, bay leaves and vinegar to pan and simmer until reduced by half.

- Strain sauce, discard solids and return liquid to pan. Add any juices that have collected under the chicken and cook until reduced to 1 cup.

- Remove sauce from heat and whisk in butter to thicken.

- Serve warm or chill and serve cold. Either way, don't forget the sauce.

GETTING IT JUST RIGHT

Watch your heat. The flavors in this dish are delicate and light. Sauté the onions without browning to prevent rich caramelization from overpowering the fresh taste of tarragon and crisp white wine.

While it takes longer to finish, resist the urge to boil the chicken. A slow simmer will result in tender, moist meat, while a roiling boil makes chicken breasts that are tough, and dry—even in water!

JONATHAN BARDZIK

"I'LL TAKE THE LIGHT POTATO SALAD, PLEASE."

With each new summer cookout looms the threat that someone is going to show up with those clear plastic containers from the deli counter of potato salad, macaroni salad and coleslaw. Now, rumor has it that these salads actually contain potatoes, macaroni and cabbage, but the protective coating of mayonnaise obscures any possible proof.

Okay, that was a bit of hyperbole, but most summer cookouts abound with rich, grilled meats and sauces, toasted buns and baskets of chips and dip. What I want from my salad is something light and bright to balance the plate, and a gloopy heap of mayonnaise just doesn't cut it. Enter the "French" potato salad.

Like may other American "French" delicacies—fries, toast and dressing—I'm not sure how French this is, but I think they would approve. Boiled potatoes are tossed, still warm, in a sharp, buttery vinaigrette, with garlic or shallots and fresh herbs. They soak up the dressing and release the flavorful oils from the greens; exactly what you want sitting next to your burger, hanger steak or chicken thighs, complete with flawless grill marks.

Experiment from Memorial Day to Labor Day with the freshest ingredients. Toss with halved cherry tomatoes and basil, use fresh tasting tarragon and shallots, baby arugula or minced red peppers. But please, I'll take my potato salad without mayonnaise. And I like my burgers rare.

Tip: Tossing the hot potatoes with the garlic and herbs releases their natural oils for bright, fresh flavor.

Tip: If you can't find fingerlings, use another low-starch potato like baby reds or Yukon Gold.

french potato and tomato salad

Serves 6-8

With summer's smoky, rich, grilled meats, breads and starchy vegetables like corn, skip the fatty mayo and use a light vinaigrette for pasta and potato salads. It holds up better under outdoor heat, too.

Ingredients:

2 pounds fingerling potatoes

4 tbs fresh, chopped herbs like tarragon, basil, parsley and chives

2 cloves garlic, minced

1 pint cherry or grape tomatoes, halved

For dressing:

2 cloves garlic, minced

1/3 cup Champagne vinegar

1 tsp dijon mustard

2/3 cups olive oil—the good stuff!

Directions:

- Boil potatoes in salted water. When they are easily pierced with a knife, with a little resistance remaining in the center, drain.

- Toss together herbs and minced garlic in a large bowl.

- Make dressing: Mash garlic into a paste with coarse salt by dragging it across your cutting board with the flat side of your knife.

- Place garlic paste in a small bowl with vinegar and mustard. Season with pepper.

- Pour the oil into the dressing in a thin stream, while whisking. This will form a creamy emulsion.

- When just cool enough to handle, cut potatoes into 1" pieces and toss in bowl with herbs and garlic.

- Dress salad to coat with 2/3 cups vinaigrette. Set potatoes aside for 15-20 minutes to absorb dressing.

- Toss tomatoes into salad and add additional dressing as needed. Season to taste with salt, pepper and additional fresh herbs as needed.

WHEN IS A POTATO NOT A POTATO?

Like squash or tomatoes, we rarely think of potatoes as being distinctly different from one type to the next. You know a Yukon Gold has less starch than a Russet, but what about its flavor? The fingerling potatoes in this recipe are firm and creamy, perfect for a light, summery salad. Want to blow your mind? Track down purple Peruvian potatoes or the boldly-flavored Eva, introduced by Cornell University.

JONATHAN BARDZIK

Tip: How do you seed a cucumber? Cut it in half lengthwise and run a spoon down the middle, scraping out the seeds.

creamy cold cucumber soup

Serves 6-8

There's nothing better on hot summer nights. Light and easy, bright with fresh summer herbs, mellowed by whole yogurt, you'll feel cooler with every bite.

Ingredients:

1 shallot, peeled

2 cloves garlic, peeled

4 large cucumbers, peeled and seeded

2 cups whole yogurt, plain

1 tbs finely chopped mint

2 tbs chopped dill

1 cup cold water

Juice of 1 lemon

Diced onion and cucumber for garnish

Directions:

- Using a microplane, grate the shallot and garlic into a large bowl.

- Using a box grater, grate the cucumbers over the same bowl.

- Stir in the yogurt and fresh herbs.

- Add water to dilute to desired consistency. You may not need the entire cup.

- Season to taste with lemon juice, salt and pepper. You may not need to use all of the juice. Add a tablespoon or two at a time.

- Garnish with diced onions and cucumbers.

PUTTING IT TOGETHER:

Fresh from the farm

Your trip to the farm market was about all the excitement you can handle today. Enjoy summer's best—crisp cucumbers, bright, juicy heirloom tomatoes and sugary corn—without ever turning on the stove.

» Creamy Cold Cucumber Soup

» Tomato Salad with Pesto Balsamic Vinaigrette

» Herbed Goat Cheese Corn Salad

JONATHAN BARDZIK

I DIDN'T USED TO LIKE TOMATOES

I feel like I should be sitting in a confessional, leaning in close, talking directly to the camera.

"I didn't used to like tomatoes," I would say in a hushed tone. "For years I thought raw tomatoes were gross!" Perhaps this revelation is so shocking that I should ask to be silhouetted out, my voice modulated.

It's true. As a child I hated raw tomatoes. I loved Brussels sprouts, broccoli, cabbage and cauliflower. Give me artichokes and onions, just about anything Mom put on the dinner table, but I grimaced each year when she asked me to try one bite of a ripe tomato, freshly picked as we stood in her garden.

Nine years ago that started to change and today I love raw tomatoes. I chalk it up to a wiser palate. This past week I decided to venerate the first of this summer's tomatoes, picked fresh under the hot sun. Two thick slices of beefsteak-type tomatoes didn't need anything more than salt and pepper, but I went ahead and added a simple, balsamic vinaigrette made with fresh basil pesto, fragrant from pounding in the mortar. I fell in love with tomatoes all over again. Then I called my Mom.

Tip: If the pesto gets too thick while pounding, add a tablespoon of oil to loosen it up.

tomato salad with pesto balsamic vinaigrette

Serves 6-8

Score, you just got three recipes in one!—a fresh basil pesto, a pesto vinaigrette and a wonderful, heirloom tomato salad. Toss leftover pesto with steamed squash or fresh pasta. Use the vinaigrette over grilled chicken or steaks.

For pesto:
- 2 cloves garlic, minced
- 1 1/2 cups chopped, fresh basil
- 1/4 cup toasted pine nuts
- 1/2 cup grated Parmesan cheese
- 1/4 cup olive oil—the good stuff!

For dressing:
- 2 tbs minced shallot
- 3 tbs pesto
- 2-3 tbs aged balsamic vinegar
- 1 cup olive oil—the good stuff!

For salad:
- 3 large, fresh tomatoes
- 4-6 basil leaves cut in thin ribbons

Directions:

- Make the pesto: Using mortar and pestle, pound garlic with 1/2 tsp coarse sea salt.

- Then pound in basil, followed by pine nuts, and cheese.

- Add 2 tbs oil, then more as needed to make a thick sauce. Season to taste with pepper and additional salt.

- If you don't have a mortar and pestle, put the garlic, salt, basil, pine nuts and cheese in a food processor. Pulse until finely chopped. With the motor running, drizzle in oil until sauce comes together.

- Make dressing: whisk together shallot, pesto and vinegar.

- Pour the oil into the dressing in a thin stream, while whisking. This will form a creamy emulsion. You may not need all the oil. Start with 1/2 cup and taste as you go. This is a very thick dressing.

- Season to taste with salt and pepper. Taste the dressing with a piece of tomato and correct the balance of oil, vinegar and pesto, if needed.

- Serve over thick slices of the freshest tomatoes you can find! Top with ribbons of fresh basil.

I LOVE LEFTOVERS!

No one ever complains about having too much pesto or 25-year-old balsamic vinegar in the house, but you don't even have to get creative to use up these leftovers. Mix a few tablespoons of pesto in with beef for your burgers. Top with a thick slab of the ripest, juiciest tomato you can find and drizzle on some pesto-balsamic vinaigrette.

JONATHAN BARDZIK

Tip: The "count" for shrimp refers to the number of shrimp in a pound. The higher the number, the smaller the shrimp.

Tip: Longer marinating does not always mean more flavor. Leave the shrimp in the marinade for a few hours and you end up with ceviche. Leave it overnight and the heavy acids from the citrus and vinegar will turns shrimp's delicate proteins into mush.

spicy orange soy grilled shrimp

Serves 6

These shrimp are bright and sweet. Eat them hot off the grill, or serve them with a tropical salsa, shredded cabbage, flour tortillas and plenty of cold beer! Grill extra and save them for a cold lunch the next day.

Ingredients:

1/2 cup soy sauce

1/2 tsp lime zest

1/4 tsp orange zest

1/2 cup fresh squeezed orange juice

1/2 cup lime juice, about 2 limes

1/2 cup unseasoned rice wine vinegar

2 cloves garlic, minced

3 whole scallions, thinly sliced

1 jalapeño, sliced horizontally into rounds

1/4 cup plus 2 tbs chopped cilantro

1 tbs toasted sesame oil

1/2 tsp salt

2 1/2 pounds 21-25 count shrimp

Directions:

- If using wooden skewers, soak in water.

- Whisk together all ingredients, except shrimp and 2 tbs cilantro, in a bowl.

- Peel and devein the shrimp, if needed. Place in a freezer bag and pour marinade over shrimp.

- Seal the bag, place in clean bowl, and refrigerate for 20-30 minutes.

- Remove shrimp from marinate and skewer. Pierce each one twice, so they don't spin when you turn them.

- Using a hot grill, cook shrimp off of direct heat for 2-3 minutes per side until opaque.

- Remove from heat, toss with 2 tbs fresh cilantro and serve with additional lime wedges.

PUTTING IT TOGETHER:

Coming in off the beach

Sand still between your toes (and in your suit!), you walk in off the beach, sit in the shade of an umbrella and enjoy the cool breeze. Made ahead of time, you can pull these right out of the fridge for a quick meal before your kids run back into the waves.

» Watermelon Gazpacho

» Spicy Orange Soy Grilled Shrimp—add shredded cabbage and tortillas for tacos!

» Peaches and Blueberries with Thai Basil Whipped Cream

JONATHAN BARDZIK

Tip: Macerating is the process of letting fruit release it's natural juices. A sprinkle of sugar or a splash of alcohol helps the process along.

Tip: Not a fan of black licorice? Never fear. The light, licoricey flavor of summer favorites like Italian basil, French tarragon and bulbs of fennel lends summer dishes a refreshing note that won't offend.

peaches and blueberries with thai basil whipped cream

Serves 6-8

Sweet peaches and tart blueberries are the perfect combination, warmed with ground cardamom. Hand-whipped, fresh cream infused with the spicy, licoricey taste of Thai basil makes this both light and decadent.

Ingredients:

3 peaches, sliced

2 cups blueberries

1/2 tsp ground cardamom

1 tbs sugar

2 tbs roughly chopped Thai basil

1-2 tbs sugar

2 cups heavy or whipping cream

Directions:

- Toss sliced peaches and blueberries together with cardamom and sugar. Let macerate in fridge for 30-45 minutes. If they don't release any liquid after the first 15 minutes, add a squeeze of fresh lemon juice. How liquidy this gets depends on how juicy your fruit is. Just go with it.

- On a cutting board, sprinkle the roughly chopped basil with the sugar and chop together until the basil is broken down almost as finely as the sugar.

- Whisk the cream to soft peaks. Then whisk in the basil sugar just until peaks are stiff, being careful not to over whisk.

- Serve fruit topped with a generous dollop of cream. And by "dollop" I mean "giant spoonful."

BY HAND

Equipment saves time and work, but you really get to know your ingredients when you work them by hand. You may go back to using electric beaters, but whisking cream and egg whites is how you experience that moment when the texture, volume and moisture are just right. It makes the difference between sweet, light, rich, whipped cream and its poorer, heavy, arid cousin. This is the moment you truly value the company of friends in the kitchen; because you are about to ask them to help.

JONATHAN BARDZIK

fall's first:

fresh flavors for changing seasons

AUTUMN IS FOR APPLES

I grew up in Amherst, MA, where fall is synonymous with apples. McIntosh apples to be specific. We bought them by the bagful, drank their sweet cider and ate Atkins Farms' cider donuts* (also by the bagful).

Marianne, the cook at Bement School, always had a bowl of them waiting as a snack at the end of each day. At home there were apples, too. Mom pressed fresh sauce through the food mill and baked apples in pies. My favorite though, was her apple crisp.

Fresh out of the oven it would bubble, syrupy inside and crumbly like a cookie on top. The recipe was simple and I learned it early. The card, typed out by my Grandmother, bears Mom's handwritten note: "Gram's recipe '68."

My first fall in DC, shopping at Eastern Market, I searched for a perfect McIntosh among the bounty of apples there. I finally found some, red and shiny, and sunk my teeth in for the first bite. I was disappointed.

The sharp crack, the crisp flesh and the juice running down my chin were absent. A bit of research revealed that apple varieties develop texture, sugar and juice better in some climates and soils than in others. My perfect New England apple was not to be found in the warmer fall nights of the Mid-Atlantic.

Much to my delight the farmers at Eastern Market introduced me to apples that ripen beautifully here in the Mid-Atlantic. Sweet Kiku, firm Stayman, tart Nittany. I also discovered Honeycrisp, as crisp, sweet and juicy as any Mac I have eaten, but then, everything always tastes better with a hint of nostalgia.

*I've recently learned you can order Atkins' cider donuts online. Fortunately, "bathing suit figure" isn't really an issue in the fall.

WHAT TO DRINK: WINDING DOWN, WARMING UP

Beer—Sure it's still summer, but the Germans start Octoberfest in September, so go for it! There are so many great Octoberfest beers out there. Challenge yourself and try them all. For hot days that cool down to crisp nights grab a Dunkel style beer. It's a dark German lager whose caramel flavoring drinks well with food—especially the season's last beef and pork from the grill.

Wine—Fall marks the return of red wines. Spicy, bold, easy-drinking grapes like South American Malbec, Spanish Shiraz and California Zinfandel warm up fall dinners and make a perfect bottle to open for an evening by the fire pit.

Cocktails—Cold days call for warming drinks. Mix cider, brandy, a splash of soda for a cidery-take on a Side Car. Break out blood orange bitters and shake them with bourbon over ice.

MUSIC: FOOTBALL AND FALLING LEAVES

From fight songs at the fifty-yard line to folk songs for falling leaves, fall music lets us say goodbye to summer and charge forward into the season ahead.

Yo La Tengo—*Autumn Sweater*
Death Cab For Cutie—*Grapevine Fires*
Pet Shop Boys—*My October Symphony*
Indigo Girls—*Joking*
Frank Sinatra—*Come Fly With Me*
Janelle Monáe—*Tightrope*
The Best Damn Band in the Land—*Buckeye Battle Cry*
Saint Etienne—*Woodcabin*
Morel—*If You Love Me*
Cocteau Twins—*Orange Appled*
David Gray—*Babylon*
Fleet Foxes—*Blue Ridge Mountains*
Adele—*I Can't Make You Love Me*

Tip: I always double the crumble crust, and never leave off the cream.

Tip: Taste your apples. You want a tart, baking apple, sweeter than a Granny Smith, but not as sugary as a Pink Lady or Delicious. If the apples you bring home from the farm market are too sweet, just add a squeeze or two of lemon juice.

my mom's mom's apple crisp

Serves 8

Sweet, soft, spiced apples with a thick crumble crust. The only way this gets better is when topped with homemade vanilla ice cream or a drizzle of fresh cream. This is the recipe Gram taught my Mom and the one Mom taught me.

Ingredients:

3 lbs tart apples, about 7-8, Stayman, Empire and McIntosh
   are all good choices

2 tbs butter

Fresh-squeezed lemon juice

1 cup all purpose flour

1 cup dark brown sugar

1/2 cup butter

1/2 tsp salt

1 tsp cinnamon or apple pie spice

Directions:

- Pre-heat the oven to 375 degrees.

- Peel, core and thickly slice apples.

- Pile apples in a 9x9 deep baking dish. If you want more crust go for a shallower and wider dish, and double the recipe for the topping.

- If the apples you are using seem dry top with a few pats of butter. If they seem too sweet, sprinkle with lemon juice.

- Blend the remaining ingredients. Gram used a pastry blender. My Mom pulses them in a food processor until they come together.

- Spread the topping over the apples. It will crumble a bit. No worries.

- Bake the apple crisp for thirty minutes or until the apples are done. The apples should be super soft.

- Serve hot or cold with or without cream.

PUTTING IT TOGETHER:

Dinner after the soccer game

Win or lose, whether you're running around the field or cheering from the sides, an afternoon of soccer works up an appetite.

» Cider and Mustard
   Brussels Sprout Slaw

» Fennel Crusted Pork

» Apple Crisp

JONATHAN BARDZIK

Tip: Boiling vegetables until crisp-tender and shocking them in ice water to stop the cooking is called blanching. It's a great way to take the raw edge off of vegetables like green beans, asparagus and broccoli for a crudités platter.

cider and mustard brussels sprout slaw

Serves 6-8

Who knew Brussels sprouts could taste light and fresh? This salad just gets better over time as the dressing lightly wilts the slaw. The sharp vinaigrette blends with salty-rich pancetta and the earthy sprouts.

Ingredients:

4 cups Brussels sprouts, about 1 pound, bottoms trimmed and halved

1/2 cup plus 1 tbs olive oil—the good stuff!

1/2 cup diced pancetta

1 shallot, minced

1/3 cup apple cider vinegar

2 tbs sharp, grainy mustard

Directions:

- Add Brussels sprouts to salted, boiling water and cook for 1 minute until bright green. Remove and place in an ice bath—a mix of 50% water and 50% ice. When sprouts are cool, drain and pat dry.

- Warm 1 tbs oil in a small skillet over medium heat. Sauté pancetta until crispy. Remove to drain on paper towels. Thinly slice Brussels sprouts and place in a bowl with enough room to toss with the dressing.

- Whisk together shallot, apple cider vinegar and mustard, with salt and pepper to taste.

- Pour remaining ½ cup oil into the dressing in a thin stream, while whisking. This will form a creamy emulsion.

- Dress Brussels sprouts with half of the dressing and all of the pancetta. Let rest 5-10 minutes and season to taste with additional dressing as needed.

AWARD-WINNING

I have already earned cooking's top honor. It was presented by Tina, who together with her son, Archer, regularly visits my farm market cooking demos. The week in question, I was cooking Brussels sprouts: blanched, sliced thinly and tossed in a vinaigrette.

Even among the most adventurous of the under-five-year-old dining set, these small, cabbage-y tasting treasures are rarely tolerated, much less beloved. Saturday morning, however, Archer reached for seconds. If that wasn't enough, his mom said, "he eats every vegetable you cook, you can't seem to go wrong...and you can share that."

So I do, glowing with pride. And to prove that I have a heart, I served Archer pumpkin pancakes the very next Saturday. He earned it.

JONATHAN BARDZIK

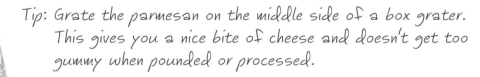

Tip: Grate the parmesan on the middle side of a box grater. This gives you a nice bite of cheese and doesn't get too gummy when pounded or processed.

Tip: Toast walnuts over low heat in a small fry pan. Watch carefully, nuts burn quickly. They are ready when golden and lightly fragrant.

arugula walnut pesto

Makes about 1 1/2 cups pesto
Cold nights end summer's basil, but nutty, peppery arugula grows most of the winter in farmers' cold frames. Make it by hand for bragging rights. Toss with fettuccine and grilled chicken for a one-dish meal.

Ingredients:

1 clove garlic, roughly chopped

1 cup chopped toasted walnuts

3/4 cups freshly grated Parmesan cheese (see tip)

2 cups arugula, loosely packed

1-2 tbs olive oil—the good stuff!

Directions:

This can be made either by hand in a mortar and pestle, or in a food processor.

By hand:

- Add garlic and a pinch of coarse salt to the mortar. Pound garlic into a paste.

- Add walnuts to garlic paste and pound until it looks like thick, chunky peanut butter.

- Add the Parmesan cheese and pound until incorporated. If the paste gets too thick, add a teaspoon of oil.

- Add the arugula a handful at a time and pound away. Add more when you have room in your mortar.

- Add cracked pepper to taste. Start with 5-6 grinds and go from there.

- Add olive oil to thin and bind. Start with a tablespoon. You shouldn't need more than two. Season to taste with additional salt and pepper.

In a food processor:

- Add garlic, walnuts and cheese to a food processor. Pulse until chopped together, about 4-6 three second pulses.

- Add arugula and process until coarsely blended. Keep it rustic as opposed to puréed.

- Remove pesto to a bowl. Stir in pepper, salt and olive oil.

GETTING IT JUST RIGHT

You won't find a mortar and pestle in every kitchen, but if you do, it was likely a wedding gift, or a present from mom. It's sitting up on a shelf filled with a couple utensils, or a small houseplant, gathering dust. I've started leaving mine, clean and empty, out on the counter. It's within reach when I need to grind the white peppercorns that aren't in a mill, or for freshly toasted cumin—which is amazing—and you will love the texture it gives this pesto. Now go thank your mom.

JONATHAN BARDZIK

Tip: Adding liquid to a pan, bringing it to a simmer and scraping up the brown bits is called "deglazing." Those caramelized brown bits are *pure flavor!*

butternut squash pancetta soup

Serves 6-8

Salt-cured, Italian pancetta lacks bacon's smoke, letting the sweet, mild taste of butternut squash shine through.

Ingredients:

1/4 pound pancetta, diced

2 tbs olive oil

1 medium onion, diced

1 clove garlic, minced

1 butternut squash, peeled and cubed, about 2-3 cups

5 sprigs thyme

2 bay leaves

5 cups chicken or vegetable stock

2 tbs maple syrup

2 tbs butter

Sherry vinegar

1 cup finely diced Honeycrisp or McIntosh apple

2 tbs chopped parsley

Directions:

- In a 4 quart soup pot, warm 1 tbs olive oil over medium-low heat. Sauté pancetta until crispy and brown. Remove pancetta with a slotted spoon leaving behind the salty, fatty goodness.

- Add onions and cook until softened. Add garlic and cook one minute longer until fragrant.

- Stir in squash. Cook until onions and squash begin to caramelize on the bottom of the pan. Don't worry if it sticks to the pan, just be careful not to let it burn.

- Add 1 cup stock, raise heat to medium-high. As the stock simmers, scrape up the brown bits from the bottom of the pan.

- Add the remaining stock, bay leaves and thyme. Simmer over medium-high heat until squash is soft. About 20 minutes.

- Remove bay and thyme and process the soup. You can use an immersion blender, but a food mill, if you have one, produces a beautiful, smooth texture.

- Finely mince the reserved, cooked pancetta. Stir into the soup and cook 5 minutes more to let the flavors blend.

- Add 2 tbs maple syrup, butter and a splash of vinegar.

- Season to taste with salt, pepper and additional syrup and vinegar as needed.

- Garnish with apple and parsley.

PUTTING IT TOGETHER:

The first frost

Fall's killing frosts wipe away the last of summer's bright flowers and bright basil. Celebrate fall on this crisp night with the season's last tomatoes and fresh flavors from your autumn garden.

» Butternut Squash Pancetta Soup

» Fettuccine with Walnut Arugula Pesto and Grilled Chicken

» Tomato Braised Fennel

JONATHAN BARDZIK

105

TRUTH OR DARE

"I really love this pear butter," Nancy stated at one of my first Saturday morning cooking demos at Washington, DC's Eastern Market. Then asked "Can you freeze it?"

I just stood there, trapped, like a deer in the headlights. Nancy had struck upon my greatest fear, that my lack of professional training would reveal me as a complete sham.

I said the only thing I could. "I don't know. It never lasts that long in our house."

It was the right answer, for three reasons. First, Nancy laughed. Secondly, it was honest. I wish I could claim moral superiority, but

the truth is that I talk a lot and have a poor memory. As Mark Twain said, "If you tell the truth, you don't have to remember anything."

The third reason is the most important. Left without an answer, Nancy went home and froze some pear butter. The next Saturday she reported that it does, in fact, freeze quite well. This is the secret to gaining great knowledge: freely and confidently admitting ignorance. Well, that and a little charm.

Tip: If you use a food mill, you don't have to peel the fruit.
If you use a food processor you do. (You're ordering
a food mill online right now, aren't you?)

savory pear butter

Serves 6-8

This is pure fall. Sugary pears, rich balsamic vinegar, earthy rosemary, warmed by cardamom and nutmeg. This freezes well according to my friend Nancy. It never lasts that long in our house. This is wonderful with roasted meats and pairs beautifully with creamy bleu cheeses like German-produced Cambozola.

Ingredients:

2 tbs butter

1 shallot, finely diced

1/8 tsp fresh grated nutmeg

1/4 tsp cardamom

1/8 tsp white pepper

5 medium Bartlett pears, chopped, about 2 1/2 cups,
    Red Bartletts if you can find them!

1 apple, chopped, like Honeycrisp or McIntosh

1 cup apple cider

1 tsp Balsamic vinegar

2 tsp chopped, fresh rosemary

Directions:

- In a small sauté pan, melt butter over medium-low heat.

- Add shallot and sauté until soft, about 5 minutes.

- Add nutmeg, cardamom and white pepper. Cook 30 seconds until fragrant.

- Add pears, apples, and cider. Turn heat to medium and cook until very soft, 10-15 minutes.

- Process mixture in food mill or blender.

- Return to pan with vinegar and rosemary. Cook an additional five minutes until thickened. Season to taste with salt and lemon juice as needed.

GET FRESH WITH ME

Once you grate or grind a spice, the fresh flavors begin to degrade. Some spices, like cinnamon, hold up pretty well. Others, like nutmeg, simply can't compare to the bright, bite of freshly grated. Toasted cumin gives off a smokey warmth when freshly browned in a pan and mill-ground. Once you taste it, you'll never go back.

Tight on time? A good old fashioned mortar and pestle makes quick work of everything from caraway and coriander to fennel and dill. Keep peppercorns in a mill on the counter and always use fresh-cracked.

JONATHAN BARDZIK

Tip: I always forget the pan is still hot from the oven and
have burned my hand (not badly). Leave an oven mitt on
the handle as a reminder that it's hot!

Tip: To clean your spice grinder, add a cubed slice of day old bread
and pulse it into fine crumbs. Wipe out the bowl with a paper towel
and it's ready for another home blend, or your morning coffee.

fennel crusted pork loin

Serves 6-8

Simple and delicious. It's as good served hot from the oven on a fall night as it is served cold at a summery September picnic. The cardamom beautifully echoes the flavors in the Savory Pear Butter.

Ingredients:

2 tbs fennel seeds

1 tsp sea salt

1/4 tsp cardamom

2 pork tenderloins

2 tbs olive oil

1 shallot, minced

1/2 tsp whole peppercorns

1 bay leaf

2 sprigs thyme

1/4 cup brandy

1 1/2 cups chicken or vegetable stock

2 tbs cold butter

Directions:

- Place fennel seeds, sea salt and cardamom in a spice grinder or coffee mill. Blend into a fine powder.

- Pat tenderloins dry and coat with ground spices.

- Heat oven to 400 degrees.

- Warm oil in a large oven-safe skillet over medium-high heat. Add pork to hot skillet and sear on all sides. About 8-10 minutes total.

- Place skillet, with seared pork, in oven and cook to 145 degrees, about 15 minutes. Remove pork from oven and reserve on a plate, tented in foil.

- Make the pan sauce: Place the skillet over medium heat. If the skillet is dry, add one tbs olive oil and the shallot. Cook until shallot is softened.

- Add peppercorns, bay and thyme to skillet along with brandy. Reduce brandy to about 1 tbs and add stock.

- Reduce stock by half and add any juices that have accumulated under the pork. Reduce sauce to 3/4 cup, remove from heat and whisk in butter.

- Serve sliced pork with sauce.

GIVE IT A REST!

Want to cook better meat? Here is the silver bullet answer: Always let meats rest before carving. Burgers off the grill and pork tenderloins from the oven benefit from 5-10 minutes. Give a large rib roast or a four-pound bird 15-20. Your Thanksgiving turkey can happily sit for a half hour.

Why the wait? Resting lets juices reabsorb to the center of your meat. Otherwise, they will run out all over your cutting board, taking delicious flavor with them and leaving your dinner dry. You will lose a little liquid while your meat waits, tented under foil. Let it rest, sitting on a platter so you can use the juices in a sauce or drizzle them over your carved prize.

JONATHAN BARDZIK

WHAT I HAVEN'T COOKED YET

Last fall at Eastern Market, one of the farmers I regularly shop with gave me a Cinderella pumpkin, saying, "I bet you haven't cooked this yet." He was right. I've cooked Blue Hubbards, warty Peanut pumpkins and dark-green, lumpy, Italian Marina de Chioggia. But I had never cooked a Cinderella pumpkin.

The first thing I wanted to know was how it tasted. Grey and oblong, Blue Hubbards are sweet and rich. If you want classic pumpkin, for pie or soup, Hubbard is the squash for you. Peanut pumpkins, also know by their French name, Galeux d'Eysines, are mild and sugary. The "peanuts" are the result of sugars building up under the skin. Chioggia, on the Adriatic coast of Italy, is known for its candy-striped beets and it's namesake pumpkin. Sweet, rich, drier and dense, it is the pumpkin of choice for gnocchi.

The Cinderella pumpkin, red and flat, is a French heirloom also known as Rouge vif D'Etampes. By some accounts, it was the pumpkin the Pilgrims and Wampanoags served at the first Thanksgiving. It is mild and not particularly sugary. It cooks down into a beautiful bright orange purée, tasting more like dinner than dessert.

The orange pumpkins we think of first are best left on our front steps, right where they belong.

Tip: No gingerbread spice on hand? Mix together 1/2 tsp each cinnamon and ginger along with 1/8 tsp each ground anise or fennel and cloves.

Tip: Stirring some of the egg white into the batter lightens it so that you don't lose volume while folding in the rest. This keeps your pancakes nice and light.

pumpkin pancakes with bacon infused maple syrup

Serves 6

Sure they're decadent—sweet syrup infused with salty bacon running down stacks of pancakes rich with pumpkin and whole milk, lightened with beaten egg whites and bright with gingerbread spices. You've been choking down dry oatmeal and egg whites every morning this week just so you could enjoy this moment. Indulge!

Ingredients:

3 thick slices bacon, diced	1 tsp gingerbread spice
2 cups real maple syrup	1 1/2 cups whole milk
1 1/2 cups all-purpose white flour	1 cup Kabocha or Hubbard squash, cooked & mashed
3 tbs sugar	4 large eggs, separated
2 tsp baking powder	1/4 cup farm fresh butter, melted
Pinch of salt	1 tsp vanilla

Directions:

- Fry bacon in a skillet until cooked through. Drain on paper towels and chop finely. Reserve bacon fat.
- Place bacon and syrup in a small saucepan and simmer.
- Mix dry ingredients—flour, sugar, baking powder, salt and gingerbread spice—and whisk lightly to combine.
- Mix wet ingredients—milk, squash and egg yolks—and whisk gently to combine.
- Whisk egg whites to stiff, but not dry, peaks.
- Gently whisk dry and wet ingredients together. It will be thick.
- Stir 1/4 whisked egg whites into the batter. Fold in the remaining egg whites.
- Using reserved bacon fat, cook one small pancake over medium heat to check seasoning. Cook remaining pancakes, using 1/4 cup batter for each.
- Serve with bacon infused syrup.

GETTING IT JUST RIGHT

For me, perfect pancakes are light and airy, preferably stacked tall. The fresh pumpkin in this recipe weighed our pancakes down, leaving them deliciously rich but heavy. The solution came in separating our eggs. The whites, whisked to stiff peaks and gently folded into the batter gave us the pillowy lightness we sought.

Why gingerbread spice? While easier to find, the familiar flavors of just cinnamon or nutmeg left these tasting a bit one-note, like a scented candle. The exotic, cool flavors of cloves and anise give our pumpkin depth, balancing its rich, roasted flavor.

JONATHAN BARDZIK

COOKING YOUR PUMPKIN

Method #1: Roasting

- Quarter your pumpkin and scoop out the seeds.

- Rub inside with olive or vegetable oil and roast at 400 degrees until the flesh can be easily pierced, through to the skin, with a fork.

- Remove from oven, let cool, and scrape pumpkin flesh from the skin.

Method #2: Stove top

- Quarter your pumpkin and scoop out the seeds.

- Peel the skin with a vegetable peeler or knife.

- Cut into a 1/2" dice.

- Warm 2 tbs olive oil in a large pan or 6 quart soup pot.

- Add pumpkin and cook until pieces begin to brown on edges.

- Add 1/4 cup water at a time as needed until pumpkin cooks down into a smooth purée, mashing as it softens.

Pumpkin freezes beautifully so you can enjoy soups, pies and decadent pancakes all winter long. It's also awesome in quesadillas with spicy sausage and sharp cheddar cheese.

117

Tip: Heating the milk to a simmer before adding
it to the cooked butter and flour makes
lumps less likely.

the best cheese sauce ever!

Makes about 2 cups
Serve this cheesy goodness over anything—broccoli, cauliflower, roasted Brussels sprouts, and omelets are a great start. The sherry and Gruyère add a nice sharp balance to the rich milk and cheddar.

Ingredients:

3 tbs unsalted butter

3 tbs flour

2 cups whole milk

Nutmeg

White pepper

1 cup shredded cheddar cheese

1/2 cup shredded Gruyère cheese

2 tbs dry sherry

Cayenne pepper

Directions:

- Melt butter over low heat in a 1 quart saucepan. Stir in flour and cook for 2-3 minutes, being careful not to let the mixture brown.

- Pour in milk, whisking briskly to avoid lumps.

- Cook an additional 15-20 minutes, stirring often, until thickened.

- Season to taste with nutmeg and white pepper. Stir in cheese until smooth. Add dry sherry

- Season to taste with cayenne, salt and pepper and additional sherry if needed.

PUTTING IT TOGETHER:
Closing up the cottage

Cold nights mark time to drain the pipes, close the shutters and bid goodbye to summer cottages until next year. After a last walk on the beach, or hike around the pond, settle in for something warm and comforting to close out the season.

» Fennel Crusted Pork with Savory Pear Butter

» Broccoli with the Best Cheese Sauce Ever!

» Apple Crisp with fresh cream

JONATHAN BARDZIK

119

Tip: Don't crowd your mushrooms. Sautéing browns food, giving it rich flavor. Without room for water to evaporate quickly, mushrooms end up soggy, braising in their own liquid.

hearty cauliflower
mushroom stew

Serves 8

Vegetarian diners shouldn't be relegated to sad plates of under-seasoned pasta with over-cooked vegetables. This stew is rich and satisfying. The carnivores at the table will never miss the meat. Serve as a one-dish meal or with a peppery arugula salad in a sharp Champagne vinaigrette.

Ingredients:

2 tbs butter

2 cups sliced Crimini mushrooms

1/4 cup dry Vermouth

1 tbs chopped, fresh thyme

1 tbs olive oil

1 medium onion, diced

2 cloves garlic, minced

1/2 tsp anchovy paste

3 Yukon Gold potatoes cut in a
  1/2" dice

3 cups vegetable stock

1/2 large head cauliflower, cut in
  florets, about 3 cups

2 sprigs fresh thyme

2 tbs bold-flavored olive oil

Nutmeg

Directions:

• Melt butter over medium heat in large sauté pan. Sauté mushrooms until golden brown on edges. Deglaze pan with Vermouth, stirring up any brown bits from the bottom. Reduce liquid. Season with thyme, salt and pepper. Reserve.

• Heat olive oil in same pan. Sauté onions until translucent, add garlic and anchovy paste and cook 30 seconds.

• Add potatoes and cook until the onion begins to brown on edges. Stir in the stock, cover and cook until potatoes have started to soften. About 15 minutes.

• Add cauliflower and fresh thyme. Cover and cook until cauliflower is crisp tender, 7-10 minutes longer.

• Uncover and let broth thicken, 5-10 minutes longer. Season to taste with olive oil, salt, pepper and nutmeg.

EWWWWWW!

You're freaked about the anchovy paste, aren't you? Your nose is wrinkled in disgust at the thought of it, fishy, salty and grey, oozing like toothpaste from a tube. Anchovy paste adds necessary layers of flavor in a dish that might otherwise feel one-dimensional. You won't taste it, I promise. It's one of those perfect stealth ingredients, delivering lots of flavor without getting caught. So go ahead, squeeze a little in, and don't tell your kids or your picky eater of a boyfriend. They'll never know.

JONATHAN BARDZIK

121

Tip: Fennel has a tough, cone-shaped core at the base.
Remove it before slicing the fennel.

Tip: Don't worry if your fennel gets a bit too soft.
The breadcrumbs will add a nice crunch.

tomato braised fennel

Serves 6

Slow cooked, crisp, licoricey fennel turns mild and rich, a perfect balance with the last tomatoes of the season. Serve alongside roast pork or a meaty white fish like Sablefish or Arctic Char.

Ingredients:

2 tbs olive oil

1/2 medium onion, diced

2 tomatoes, cored and diced

2 fennel bulbs, quartered and
    cut in 1/4" slices

White pepper

For breadcrumbs:

2 tbs olive oil

2 cloves garlic, minced

1 tsp lemon zest

2 tbs, chopped parsley

1-1 1/2 cups Panko breadcrumbs

Directions:

- Warm oil in a 3 quart sauté pan over medium heat. Add onion and cook until softened.

- Add tomatoes, cover and cook until softened, about 5 minutes.

- Stir in sliced fennel. Cover and cook until softened but still crisp, another 7-10 minutes.

- Uncover and cook until liquid evaporates and tomato thickens. Season to taste with salt and white pepper.

- While fennel finishes cooking, heat oil for breadcrumbs in a small skillet over medium-low heat. Sauté garlic until softened and golden.

- Add lemon zest and parsley and cook for 30 seconds longer. Add Panko breadcrumbs, mix in herbs and garlic, and toast until golden. Season with salt and pepper.

- Serve fennel topped with Panko.

PUTTING IT TOGETHER:

Apple picking at the orchard

A crisp morning gave way to filling baskets under late summer's still-hot sun. Now tonight's cold frost and a warm fire call for a hearty dinner. And dessert? The spoils of the day's harvest.

» Hearty Cauliflower
    Mushroom Stew

» Tomato Braised Fennel

» Warm Apple Crisp

JONATHAN BARDZIK

SIMPLE. SPECIAL.

Two weeks before Jason and I sent out wedding invitations, we sat in the kitchen with my parents, working on the guest list. The forced ranking of friends and family in order to hit a budget seemed callous, stripping the joy from this magic event.

There was no question that all family members were invited, but that was 64 guests on our side alone. The four of us winced at the prospect of choosing between new friends, old friends, and good friends of the family.

"Let's invite them all," Dad finally said. "The worst thing that can happen is they all say 'yes.' Then we order more tables and dishes and figure out how to cram everyone under the tent."

Mom nodded in agreement.

What I'm sharing in this book I learned at home. Dad, always up early, often collected flowers from our gardens and arranged them for Mom. It was in her kitchen that I first learned the comfort of simple summer recipes.

Entertaining was generous and easy—at least they made it look that way—and there was always another seat at the table. This is probably why Jason and I almost never eat alone, often inviting guests mere hours before serving a meal.

I taught them a few things, too: Billie Holliday is the perfect soundtrack for every summer dinner. Garden vegetables shine with a pat of butter and a splash of vinegar. Elegant entertaining is never farther away than a bag of tea lights.

Most importantly, my parents taught me that every day, every meal, can and should be a special occasion. One that is best shared with those we love.

Thank you Mom and Dad. I love you.

—*jonathan*

NOTHING GREAT IS DONE ALONE

Thank you to Joe Judge who inspired this journey; to Ali Bennett, for strength and perspective; to the team: Nancy Mendrala and Sam Armocido; to everyone at my home at Eastern Market: Dan Donahue at Agora Farms, Marvin and Josh Ogburn at Long Meadow Farms, Renee Shields-Farr and her team at Sapore Oil and Vinegar, Emilio and Carlos Canales at Canales Quality Meats, Barry Margeson and Katrina Cuffey, José Canales at Canales Deli, Jorge Canales at Eastern Market Grocery, Cinda Sebastian and Jesse at Gardener's Gourmet, David and Valerie Fowler at Sunny Side Farms, Noah and Tim Ashton at Ashton Farms, and Mike Bowers at Bowers Fancy Dairy; to Eric Wahl, my kitchen companion, for his rich palate and quick hands, Jonathan Schenck, Louis McClelland and all who have helped with demos; to Andrew Lightman who made me a better writer; to those in my second home in Columbus, OH, Robin Davis, author and food editor at the Columbus Dispatch, Ben Walters at Spices LTD, Tammie Main at Fearless Flavors; to Darren Santos who memorialized our friends, family and wedding, to Jenny Lehman who captured a morning at Eastern Market, to Angela Treadwell-Palmer and Garry Grueber for the beautiful flowers; Seth Semons' eagle eyes; Jessie Judge, who made my name look cool; Bob Dolibois and Michael Geary for their gift of time and vision; Jim Boynton who listened and advised; Mike Jasinski and Jennifer Polanz, my beer buddies; Joe Novotny, Cliff Hunter, Mike Schmidt and Matt Fulgham who keep me rocking; to Peter Glöege, who turned recipes, stories and photos into this beautiful book, and to David Hazard for inspiration and invaluable, professional counsel.

There are many others who have been invaluable, from offering advice to making a recipe recommendation. Please know you are appreciated.

Finally, my sincere thanks to everyone who has attended a demo, commented on a Face-

THE STORY OF THESE PICTURES

Just over a year ago, our friend Sam came over for dinner one night, after seeing my Eastern Market cooking demo. At the end of the meal he said, "I want to learn how to cook." Living on his own for the first time, he was getting tired of cereal, PB&J and pasta.

I invited Sam to join me the following week when I developed new recipes for my Saturday cooking demo. We talked about knife skills, tasted infused vinegars and Amish butter, and talked about the flavor profile of zucchini, cilantro and tomatoes. Sam returned the following week, and the week after.

One of those first weeks, when I struggled to get the camera to capture the bright colors of a peach salsa, Sam offered his help. "I used to do some photography in college," he said. Two weeks later he showed up with $2,000 worth of camera equipment that had been gathering dust in his apartment, and changed the way we photograph food.

His first images were beautiful and they just keep getting better. Sam's involvement in the recipe development process results in pictures that tell a story about flavor, ingredients and technique, and go well beyond culinary glamour shots (although these pics are hot!).

Oh, and Sam can cook now. Really well. His Mom told me so.

JONATHAN BARDZIK

127

Photo by Ray LaVoie

JONATHAN BARDZIK

is a cook, storyteller, and writer living in Washington, DC. Originally from western Massachusetts, he is self-trained from nearly two decades of reading, testing, and sharing his passion for cooking and food with family and friends. He loves most to learn about new ingredients, recipes, and techniques.

In 2011, Jonathan began sharing his love of cooking at Washington, DC's historic Eastern Market, where he provides weekly demonstrations using fresh ingredients from the Market's local farmers and purveyors. Growing up in the horticulture industry gives Jonathan a special connection to farmers and their farms (and explains his nerdy attachment to members of the Brassica family).

Jonathan is a regular contributing food writer to Capitol Community News' publications the Hill Rag and Mid City DC. When not cooking at Eastern Market, food events and in people's homes, Jonathan can be found at home with his husband Jason, cooking for friends and family in their kitchen.

Jonathan is often asked, "What is your favorite thing to cook?" The answer has inspired a blog and Facebook page called What I Haven't Cooked Yet, online at www.jonathanbardzik.com, where he shares his recipes and adventures in the kitchen.